## DATE DUE

| | | | |
|---|---|---|---|
| DANA NOV 19 1964 | | | |
| Feb 10 | | | |
| APR 5 1967 | | | |
| Feb 16 | | | |
| JUL 2 1974 | | | |
| APR 16 1975 | | | |
| MAY 25 1984 | | | |
| JUN 26 1998 | | | |
| NOV 10 1998 | | | |
| | | | |
| | | | |
| | | | |
| | | | |
| | | | |
| | | | |
| | | | |
| GAYLORD | | | PRINTED IN U.S.A. |

# STATE BIRDS
# and FLOWERS

## by *Olive L. Earle*

WILLIAM MORROW & COMPANY, NEW YORK, 1961

# INDEX

In some states there is no official choice of a state bird and state flower. Where this is the case changes may occur and conflicting statements are sometimes made. The following list is based on information available in 1960. (X) indicates unofficial choice.

The bald eagle has been our national bird since 1782, when the design for the great seal of the United States was chosen. There is no official national flower, but on the seal an olive branch with thirteen leaves and thirteen berries is held by the eagle. Olive branches are part of the insignia of the United Nations also.

Each of the forty-eight states has a flower and a bird to represent it. Usually the choice has been made by general consent or by the votes of schoolchildren. In most states, the choice has been made official by state legislation. Some flowers and birds have been selected by more than one state. An example of this is the mockingbird, state bird of five different states. The mockingbird is pictured and described under Arkansas on Page 9. The names of the four other states are listed on Page 9, and small marginal drawings show the flowers of those five states.

# ALABAMA

The yellowhammer, or flicker, be- **5** longs to the woodpecker family. He chisels a nest hole in a tree with his strong bill. He has a tree climber's foot — two of the toes point backward. Unlike other woodpeckers, the flicker spends much time on the ground in open places. There, with his long probing bill, he hunts for cut worms and grubs or for his favorite food, ants. He collects them on his barbed, sticky tongue. Sometimes he explores the bark of trees for insects. A flicker is easy to recognize. When flying, he exposes a white shirttail and shows a yellow lining under the wings and tail. The back is brown, barred with black; the light under parts are freckled with black spots. The back of the gray head has a bright red stripe, and a black crescent is on the breast. Various calls are used by the flicker. One is the prolonged laugh—"Wick-wick-wick-wick!" Often he drums loudly on a dead tree with his bill. Other names: Highhole, golden-winged woodpecker.

Flower: *Goldenrod. See page 24.*

Montgomery

# ALASKA

**6** The forget-me-not grows wild all over the world. Some species like to live in damp meadows or beside brooks; others make blue carpets on mountainsides. On bleak mountains the flowers are almost stemless; in sheltered areas the plant sometimes reaches eighteen inches in height. The flower, with a bright yellow eye in the center, has five notched petals of intense blue.

The willow ptarmigan belongs to the grouse group, and sometimes he is called the willow grouse. He is famous for his change of plumage. In summer the birds are a varied chestnut brown, matching the color of the ground. In winter they are white and almost invisible against a snowy background. When snow is deep on their feeding grounds, they move, often in great flocks, to brush-grown riversides and coastal areas, where they can find willow and alder twigs and buds to eat. The nest is a depression in the ground lined with grasses and leaves. In it seven or more eggs are laid. Both the eggs and the birds are used as food by the Eskimos.

FORGET-ME-NOT

PTARMIGAN
*17 inches*

Juneau

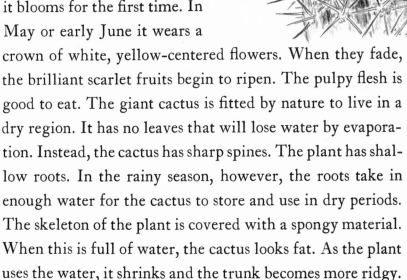

**7** The giant or saguaro cactus towers above other desert plants. Growing at the rate of not more than an inch a year, this cactus may finally reach a height of fifty feet. It is estimated that the giants live for two hundred years. When a plant is sixty or more years old, it blooms for the first time. In May or early June it wears a crown of white, yellow-centered flowers. When they fade, the brilliant scarlet fruits begin to ripen. The pulpy flesh is good to eat. The giant cactus is fitted by nature to live in a dry region. It has no leaves that will lose water by evaporation. Instead, the cactus has sharp spines. The plant has shallow roots. In the rainy season, however, the roots take in enough water for the cactus to store and use in dry periods. The skeleton of the plant is covered with a spongy material. When this is full of water, the cactus looks fat. As the plant uses the water, it shrinks and the trunk becomes more ridgy.

Phoenix
⊙

# ARIZONA

# ARIZONA

CACTUS WREN
*8½ inches*

**8** The cactus wren is the largest member of the wren family. His back is brown, barred with black and streaked with white. There is a white stripe over each eye. The bird's breast is white, spotted with black. His wings are decidedly rounded. He has no sweet song, as do many of his relatives, but he has a scolding call. The angrier he gets, the harsher his voice becomes. These energetic birds are always busy and, like some other wrens, have the habit of building extra nests. One nest will be the family nursery in which there may be from four to seven young birds. The other nests are built by the male, apparently just to keep busy. The nest is shaped like a flask lying on its side. When cold weather comes, the birds build shelter nests. The prickly cholla cactus is their favorite haunt. The desert is the home of the cactus wren. If he lived in farming country, he would be of great value, for he is a fine insect hunter. His food includes many destructive insect pests as well as a few weed seeds.

The mockingbird is this country's most famous song-  **9**
ster. In the spring he sings all day and sometimes all night.
He has his own beautiful song, but his name comes from his
ability to imitate other songs and sounds. He mocks other
birds so cleverly that even they are deceived. He can mimic
a barking dog, insect noises, and the sounds made by chickens and farm animals. Mockingbirds prefer open places and
pastures. They like company and often live in gardens near
houses. They eat berries, seeds, and insects. The general
color of the mockingbird is gray. The upper part is ash gray,
with almost black wings and tail. There is a white blotch
on each wing and white on the outer tail feathers. The very
long tail is another identifying feature. Mockingbirds are
plentiful in the Southern states. They are often seen in
northern areas during the summer,
and have been seen occasionally as
far north as New York State.

Flower: *Apple blossom. See page 31.*

MOCKINGBIRD
*10½ inches*

Little Rock

*also* FLORIDA
MISSISSIPPI
TENNESSEE
TEXAS

# CALIFORNIA

**10** The California poppy is sometimes called the golden poppy. It is brilliant yellow, shading to gold at its heart. The flower is two or three inches across and the plant grows two feet tall. Countless millions of plants paint the mountainsides in California with gold in the spring. The lengthy roots help the plant to withstand long periods of dry weather. The flower has four petals, and only in sunshine do these unfurl to show the many stamens and the pistil. After the petals have fallen, and often before, the fast-growing pistil develops a long, grooved seed pod. Sometimes the ripe pod is four inches long. Below the flower, the slender stem swells to form a rimmed pedestal for the flower parts. When the poppy is ready to open, its petals press upwards against the two sepals, which are joined to form a peaked cap. The cap is easily thrown off when loosened from its base. The leaves are finely cut and are more gray than green.

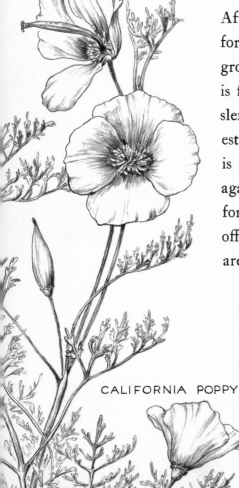
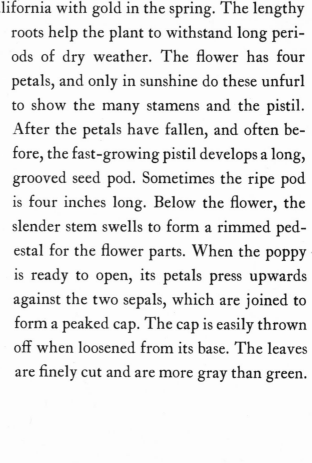

CALIFORNIA POPPY

The California quail is a bird that seems to prefer walking to flying, though he can fly fast enough when danger threatens. Groups of these birds feed together on the ground. They are largely vegetarians, but they also eat some of man's insect foes. As they feed, they chatter to each other in a great variety of phrases. At night they leave the ground to roost in low trees and bushes. The male California quail has a smoky-brown back and a bluish-gray breast. His sides have white and chestnut stripes, and there is a chestnut patch below. His headband and throat are almost black and are edged with white. His nodding crest of six curved feathers is black. The coloring of the female is much quieter, and she has a shorter crest. The fluffy chicks, twelve to sixteen in a brood, run around gaily almost as soon as they are out of their shells. The nest of grasses, in a hollow in the ground, is usually built beside a rock, stump, or similar shelter.

Sacramento

CALIFORNIA
QUAIL
*11 inches*

**12** The lark bunting, like the European skylark, sings a varied and brilliant song as he soars high in the air. He sings, too, in chorus with others of his kind, as he perches on the weed stalks of the prairie or flies over them. A soft sweet song comes from the sky when flocks of lark buntings are traveling south for the winter. The "bunting" part of his name means plump or rounded out. The bird has many popular names. White wing describes him, for both male and female have white wing patches. They are a startling contrast to the black plumage of the male. The female shows less white and is a streaked grayish brown. In winter the male wears a similar inconspicuous suit, but he keeps a small black chin patch. Lark buntings are seed eaters. The nest is on the ground. A tuft of grass or weeds gives partial shelter to the sunken nest. The outer layer is made of grass and weed stems; the lining is down from plants. When sitting on her four or five pale-blue eggs, the female's color acts as camouflage. When most birds are seeking shelter from high winds, this one flies around and seems to enjoy the buffeting.

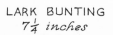

LARK BUNTING
$7\frac{1}{4}$ *inches*

Columbine grows wild in many **13** places, and many varieties, of different colors, are cultivated in gardens. The large blue-and-white columbine, measuring two inches across, is the one honored as the state flower of Colorado. Its petals are white, sometimes tinged with blue, and the sepals (which look like petals) are violet blue. The five petals form funnels, each ending in a long slender spur curving outward. These spurs contain nectar, and short-tongued insects sometimes nip holes in them in order to collect the sweet juice. The leaves, on long stems, are divided into three leaflets and are grayish green. The plant grows to a height of two feet. The columbine has a long flowering season, because new buds form on the branched stalks and open while the five-sectioned seed pods in the maturing flowers are ripening. Varying types of columbine bloom from April to July.

COLUMBINE

Denver

COLORADO

# CONNECTICUT

**14** Mountain laurel has glossy dark-green leaves which remain on the plant throughout the year. New light-green leaves and the blossoms come in May and June. The round-topped shrub may grow to fifteen feet or more in height but blooms even when it is quite small. The flowers, on short sticky stems, are rose pink when they are buds. They open into pale-pink shallow cups about three quarters of an inch across. They are set in a five-pointed calyx. The flower's pollen is distributed in an unusual way. The tips of the ten arched stamens are tucked into pockets in the cup. The slightest jar from a nectar-seeking insect releases them, and the pollen grains fly like arrows from bows. The insect guest gets well sprayed with pollen and carries it to the pistil of another flower. Grains that miss him may settle on other flower pistils in the cluster. After the flower cup falls, the base of the pistil swells into a fruit capsule. The column of the pistil remains attached to the fruit.

Bird: Robin. See page 31.

*also* PENNSYLVANIA

MOUNTAIN LAUREL

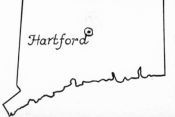

Hartford

# DELAWARE

The peach blossom is a rich deep pink. Usually the **15** tree is in full bloom before the leaves come out. The flowers are borne on the previous season's new branches only, and because they bloom very early in the year there is always danger of damage by late spring frosts. The fruit has a pulpy, juicy outer layer which covers a hard shell containing a single seed. The botanical name for fruit of this kind is *drupe*. Peach trees seldom live longer than thirty years, and though they may bear some fruit when they are quite old, it is not profitable in commercial orchards to keep trees more than seven to nine years. The mature tree is about twenty feet tall. There are many varieties of peaches, and the fruit is a favorite in many parts of the world. It is believed to have come originally from China.

The blue hen chicken is a bird that lives only in history. The legend is that in the Revolutionary War some Delaware soldiers owned fighting cocks which were the offspring of hens of a bluish color. These birds became famous for their gameness, and the men of the regiment were so courageous that they were nicknamed the "Blue Hen Chickens."

PEACH BLOSSOM

*Dover*

BLUE HEN CHICKEN

# DISTRICT OF COLUMBIA

**16** The American Beauty rose first came to public attention in 1886. Some say it was imported from France. Others believe that it was originally grown in the White House garden. The flower's rich red color, lovely fragrance, and long stem created a sensation. For many years it reigned as queen of roses, but other similar roses were created by growers and the American Beauty was pushed from her throne.

AMERICAN BEAUTY ROSE

The wood thrush likes deep woods, though many seem to prefer to sing their lovely songs around farms and in gardens. The back of the bird is varying shades of brown and its under parts are white, boldly spotted with black on the breast and sides. Wood thrushes build their nests high in trees, but they are often seen hopping along the ground, hunting for insects. They eat a little fruit, chiefly wild, but what little damage they do is paid for by their usefulness in destroying cutworms, caterpillars, beetles, and other insect pests.

Washington

WOOD THRUSH
*8 inches*

The orange blossom grows on a low-branching ever- **17** green tree, which seldom grows to be more than thirty feet high. Ripening fruit and flowers are occasionally found among the dark-green leaves at the same time. The blossoms usually have five waxy white petals surrounding numerous stamens. They have a strong fragrance. Bees visit the flowers to collect nectar for making honey of a very distinct flavor. On their visits the insects transfer pollen from tree to tree, and on one of their calls might take the pollen from one orange tree to a flower of another variety. Then the seedlings might not grow like the parent tree. To be sure of having a "true" plant, growers take buds from the variety they want and set them in the bark of a cut-back stem of a sturdy sour orange tree. The orange tree originally came from Asia. The wild ones now found in Florida are the escaped descendants of the trees brought here by the early Spanish explorers. Orange trees can stand slight frost for a brief period, but they cannot be grown in places where there is a long cold season.

Bird: *Mockingbird. See page 9.*

ORANGE BLOSSOM

# GEORGIA

Atlanta

**18** The brown thrasher has a song that gives a hint of his relationship to the mockingbird. He likes to perch on the topmost branch of a tree where, with head lifted, tail drooped, and feathers fluffed out, he sings his varied song. Except when singing, the brown thrasher spends much time on the ground, picking his insect food from among dead leaves. He eats some fruit, too. The brown thrasher is bright red brown above; dark-brown streaks mark the golden-buff under parts. His very long rounded tail is most noticeable. He thrashes or jerks it when he is excited. These birds nest in thick bushes, a few feet from the ground. They build an untidy-looking open-topped structure made of twigs, small roots, and leaves.

CHEROKEE RO:

BROWN THRASHER
*11 inches*

Georgia's cherokee rose is now a wild rose. It was brought here from China many years ago, but soon escaped from gardens to grow luxuriantly over fences and hedges. This evergreen rose's fragrant white flowers bloom in the spring.

The hibiscus has long been in cultivation because of **19** its beautiful flowers. Growers have developed a large shrub, and now there are varieties with single or double blossoms in a wide range of colors. The Hawaiian goose (nene) is the bird which represents the state.

**HIBISCUS**

There are many varieties of mock orange. The kind chosen as Idaho's state flower grows up to twelve feet in height. In early summer it is covered with masses of fragrant white flowers measuring about an inch and a half across. As in the orange blossom, glistening petals surround numerous bright yellow stamens. After the flower's four petals fall, the green seed capsule, set in a cup made by four sepals, continues to decorate the shrub. In late summer it ripens and releases the seeds. The dry seed containers look like little brown flowers, and they remain on the bush throughout the winter. Mock orange is often called syringa, which was the shrub's early botanical name.

**MOCK ORANGE**

Bird: *Mountain bluebird. See page 37.*

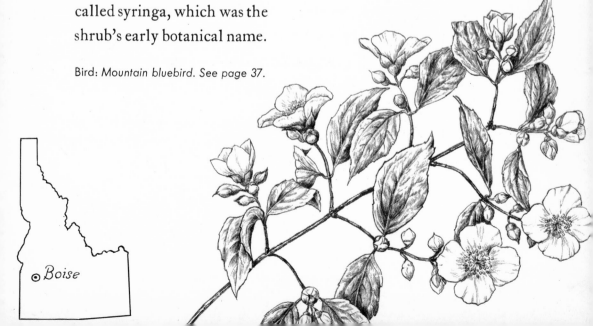

*Boise*

# ILLINOIS

**20** The cardinal is, because of his size and color, the outstanding member of the sparrow family. His color is the red of a cardinal's robe. He has an unusual beak—very large and brilliant red. Its color looks the brighter because of the black feathers that surround it, those below forming a bib, and those above joining the front of the crest. The bird expresses his feelings by erecting or lowering this crest and by his voice, which is a joyous whistle or a sharp alarm call. The cardinal's strong bill is a sign that he can crack hard seeds. He also eats a little fruit and some insects. He collects small insects for the young birds. While his mate is hatching a second set of eggs, he takes care of the first group of two, three, or four fledglings. The loose nest of twigs and stringy plant material is built in a low bush or a tangle of vines. It is lined with rootlets and, if it can be found, horsehair. The young birds have the same coloring as their mother. She is olive gray except for her wings, tail, and crest, which are a dull red. Her beak is orange red.    Flower: *Violet. See page 63.*

CARDINA
8¾ *inches*

*also* INDIANA
KENTUCK
N.CAROLIN
OHIO
VIRGINI
W.VIRGINI

Springfield

The peony has been in this country for so long that **21** it almost seems like a native plant. Actually it was brought here by early settlers, who called it the piney. Later other plants were introduced from southern Europe, Siberia, and the Far East. From them hundreds of named peonies have been developed. There are two main types—those of the bushy group that sprout at ground level and the less common tree peony that has an almost woody, erect stem growing three to four feet high. The single or the more usual double flowers are white to deepest crimson in color. In most the numerous stamens and the seed-bearing parts are hidden in the many petals. The tops of the bushy plants die as winter nears; those of the tree peonies do not. Root division provides more bushy peonies. Cuttings are taken from the tree type.

Bird: *Cardinal. See pages 20 and 62.*

*Indianapolis*

PEONY

# IOWA

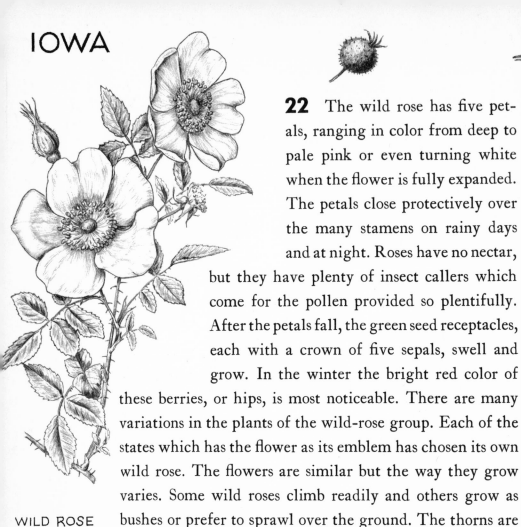

**22**  The wild rose has five petals, ranging in color from deep to pale pink or even turning white when the flower is fully expanded. The petals close protectively over the many stamens on rainy days and at night. Roses have no nectar, but they have plenty of insect callers which come for the pollen provided so plentifully. After the petals fall, the green seed receptacles, each with a crown of five sepals, swell and grow. In the winter the bright red color of these berries, or hips, is most noticeable. There are many variations in the plants of the wild-rose group. Each of the states which has the flower as its emblem has chosen its own wild rose. The flowers are similar but the way they grow varies. Some wild roses climb readily and others grow as bushes or prefer to sprawl over the ground. The thorns are stout and plentiful on the stems of some, weak and few on others. The thorns protect the plant from hungry animals and also, by acting as hooks, help the plant to climb.

WILD ROSE
*also*
GEORGIA
NEW YORK
NORTH DAKOTA

Bird: Goldfinch. See page 40.

Des Moines
⊙

# KANSAS

The sunflower is a **23** member of the composite family. The sunburst of golden banners is made up of a circle of ray flowers that attract insects to the hundreds of little brown seed-bearing disk flowers in the center. Each disk floret is a five-pointed tube. In this are five stamens which have their tips joined. The pistil, growing from the seed container, pushes against these tips and forces them out of the tube, making the pollen burst out like a yellow star. The top of the pistil then divides and its two curled-back lobes are ready to receive pollen from other florets. When the sunflower's bud opens, first the ray flowers expand, then a circle of disk flowers shows the pollen. Then the other rings of florets blossom. By the time the center ones have opened, the seeds in the outermost circle are ripening. Sunflowers grow up to ten feet tall in a single season. The heavy heads bend over and scatter the ripe seeds. Sunflowers are sometimes grown as a farm crop for the sake of the oil in the seeds. _Bird: Western meadowlark. See page 36._

SUNFLOWER

_Topeka_ ◉

# KENTUCKY

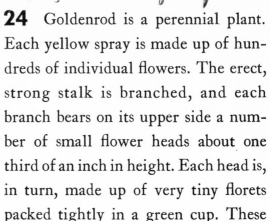

**24** Goldenrod is a perennial plant. Each yellow spray is made up of hundreds of individual flowers. The erect, strong stalk is branched, and each branch bears on its upper side a number of small flower heads about one third of an inch in height. Each head is, in turn, made up of very tiny florets packed tightly in a green cup. These miniature florets either have a banner petal to attract insects or are tube-shaped and produce the pollen and nectar prized by the visitors. Both types of florets produce seeds. As the floret fades, the fuzzy tuft growing near its base develops. It acts as a balloon, floating the ripe seed away on the wind. Often the velvety sprays remain on the plant long after frost has killed the leaves. There are more than one hundred species of goldenrod, some with heavy plumes and others with delicate sprays. Some goldenrods bloom in June; others come into bloom throughout the summer, and still others blossom in late autumn. Goldenrod is found all over this continent and is often planted as a garden flower in Europe.

Bird: *Cardinal. See pages 20 and 62.*

GOLDENROD

*also* NEBRASKA
ALABAMA

*Frankfort*

The brown pelican is a water bird. His gen- **25** eral color ranges from a chestnut to a grayish brown. His head is mainly white and a snowy strip of feathers edges his pouch. Newly hatched birds look as though covered with lamb's wool. Grown pelicans are mostly silent, but the always-hungry baby screams for his food. By thrusting his head into the pouch that hangs from his parent's lower bill, he finds a sort of soup made of partly digested fish. Waddling clumsily when he walks, the pelican flies with a graceful rhythmic wingbeat. He has a wingspread of six and a half feet. Pelicans often fly singly or in pairs, but sometimes a group flies along the seashore in a slanting single file, with an equal distance between each bird. A pelican, seeing a school of small fish in the water below, suddenly drops like a stone, making a great splash. He scoops up a fish, strains the water from his pouch, and has his meal at his leisure. Pelicans live in large colonies. The nest may be a few sticks on the ground or a well-built structure on the top of a low-growing mangrove tree.

Flower: *Magnolia. See page 33.*

**BROWN PELICAN**
*4½ feet*

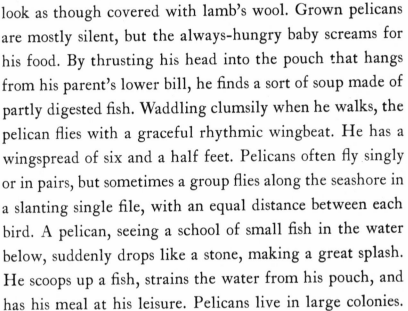

# MAINE

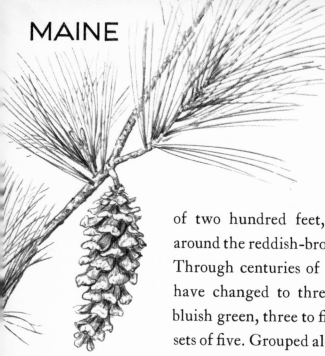

**26** The pine cone and tassel grow on the white pine, which is an evergreen tree. It grows rapidly and sometimes reaches a height of two hundred feet, with its limbs branching around the reddish-brown or grayish-brown trunk. Through centuries of evolution, the pine's leaves have changed to three-sided needles. These are bluish green, three to five inches long, and grow in sets of five. Grouped along a branch end, they form the tassel. The strongest of winds cannot harm them. Wind is necessary to pines and to many other trees, for it scatters pollen grains. The tree has two kinds of cones. The groups of small pollen bearers grow at the tips of the branches and fall off in a few weeks. The seed-bearing cones change in the course of two seasons from the green of their unripe stage to the familiar brown of the woody cone. White pine cones grow from four to ten inches long. Under each scale are two winged seeds. When fully ripe, the cones open and the falling seeds are blown far afield. Pine cones shut their scales in wet weather.

Bird: *Chickadee. See page 30.*

PINE CONE
AND TASSEL

*Augusta*

The black-eyed Susan is a com- **27** posite flower, built on the same plan as the sunflower. The ten to twenty orange-yellow ray flowers do not produce seeds. It is the dark-brown disk florets which produce them. The center cone of florets begins to blossom at its base, and day by day other circles of blossoms display their golden pollen. In the bud stage the flower head is protected by hairy green bracts. Bristles cover the strong stem and the leaves, and are a barrier against crawling insects which do not distribute pollen. But pollen is available to all the welcome flying insects, though only those with long tongues can reach the nectar deep in the tubular florets. Black-eyed Susans were originally Western flowers, but are now quite at home wherever there is a sunny field or roadside. They first traveled East mixed with clover seed when it was shipped from the West, and they spread quickly, for each flower head produces many seeds and the plant blooms from May to September. It grows to a height of three feet and the flower heads may be four inches across.

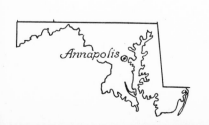

BLACK-EYED SUSAN

BALTIMORE ORIOLE
7½ *inches*

**28** The male Baltimore oriole has brilliant flame-orange plumage, accentuated by a black head, neck, upper back, and throat. The tail is black and orange and the black wings have bars of white. The coloring of the female is yellowish olive and brown. The hanging pouch-shaped nest, about seven inches deep, is built by the female. With clever knots, the framework of twine and fiber is first securely fastened. Then, working mostly from the inside and using any pliable material, she weaves a clothlike bag. A lining of hair is added. Her mate helps her by bringing building materials and whistling cheerfully. He helps feed the four to six young birds on caterpillars and other juicy insect pests. The birds were named, long ago, in honor of the black and yellow colors of Lord Baltimore, the founder of Maryland.

# MARYLAND

# MASSACHUSETTS

The trailing arbutus, or Mayflower, often blossoms **29** before the snow has melted. The plant lives close to the earth. Fallen leaves and pine needles protect its evergreen foliage in the winter. The oval leaves are dark green and the old weatherworn ones have rusty edges. After the blossoms have withered and the seeds set, fuzzy new leaves on hairy stems unfold. By degrees the old leaves decay. As they mature, the very fragrant rose-pink flowers pale to white. They grow in clusters, of a few or many, at the end of stems which branch from the woody main stem. Each flower is a slender hairy tube expanding to a five-pointed star. It measures less than half an inch across. The trailing arbutus spreads in thick mats, and it prefers either sandy soil in woods or a home among rocks under pine trees. The soil must be acid for it to thrive. Because the flowers have been carelessly picked and the roots destroyed, it is against the law in many states to gather trailing arbutus.

TRAILING ARBUTUS

# MASSACHUSETTS

**30**  The chickadee gave himself his name. "Chickadee!" he calls over and over again, very often adding extra "dee's." Occasionally he whistles a few notes. These little birds are gray in color, darker above than below, with distinctive jet-black caps and bibs. They have white cheeks and a white collar. Chickadees seem to enjoy the winter snow. They are frequent visitors at feeding stations. Hanging upside down or clinging sidewise to a piece of suet, they use their sharp beaks with energy. Being such acrobats, they can easily search the underside of a tree branch for small insects and insect eggs. For a nesting place, chickadees use a woodpecker's deserted home or any convenient hole in a fence post or tree. They fill the cavity with leaves, moss, and grass, adding a comfortable lining of feathers and other soft material. The parents may have to feed as many as eight baby birds, but when they are two weeks old the fledglings leave the crowded nest and soon learn to catch insects for themselves.

BLACK-CAPPED CHICKADEE
5¾ inches
also MAINE

The apple blossom bud is deep pink and the open **31** flowers are white streaked with pink. Five of the five-petaled blossoms are usually arranged in a circlet around a sixth one, and they are grouped on short twigs that grow along the ends of the branches. Bees and other insects carry the yellow pollen from flower to flower. The seed receptacle, with five pistils, swells and ultimately becomes the fruit.

APPLE BLOSSOM
*also* ARKANSAS

The robin arrives from the South early in the spring. The male bird sings lustily to warn other robins to keep out of his claimed area. A pair soon decide on one of a variety of locations for the bulky nest, which is made of twigs and is mud-plastered and grass-lined. The female lays from three to five blue-green eggs. Three families may be reared in the course of a summer. At first a young robin has a speckled breast instead of the familiar red. He belongs to the similarly marked thrush family.

*Lansing*

ROBIN
*10 inches*
*also* CONNECTICUT
WISCONSIN

# MINNESOTA

St. Paul

**32** The showy lady's slipper belongs to the orchid family and, like all orchids, has strange flower parts. One of this orchid's petals is enlarged to form a swollen pouch. The flower is white except for the mauve-pink pouch. A tiny bee follows inviting marks and squeezes through a narrow opening in the pouch to reach the nectar. The entrance to the pouch has downward-folding edges and cannot be used as an exit. The only way out leads the bee under one of the flower's waxy pollen masses. Grains of pollen are smeared on the back of the departing insect. They will be left on the pistil of the next showy lady's slipper visited by the bee. This large wild orchid is more than three inches long. Sometimes three flowers, one above the other, grow on the stout stem, which also bears wide leaves that are eight inches long.

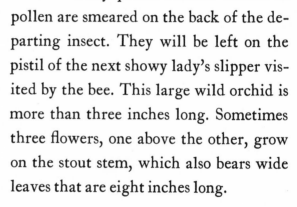

SHOWY LADY'S-SLIPPER

The magnolia **33** of the South is the most spectacular flowering tree in this country. Always green, and shaped like a pyramid, it may grow to a height of one hundred feet, with a trunk four feet thick. The long oval leaves are leathery and glossy. At the end of almost every branch the leaves form a green background for the immense white flowers, which often expand to a width of ten or twelve inches. The fragrant blossoms have six to twelve waxen petals and three sepals which look like extra petals. In the heart of the flower cup are many stamens surrounding a group of pistils. The petals fall in a few days, and the fruit begins to ripen. The seed capsules are united to form a composite fruit, shaped like a cone. When they are ripe the capsules split, and their one or two bright coral-red seeds are released. For a time these seeds remain attached, dangling by a thin thread. Magnolia trees bloom in spring and early summer. Sometimes a tree will produce a few flowers in the autumn. Bird: *Mockingbird. See page 9.*

MAGNOLIA
*Also Louisiana*

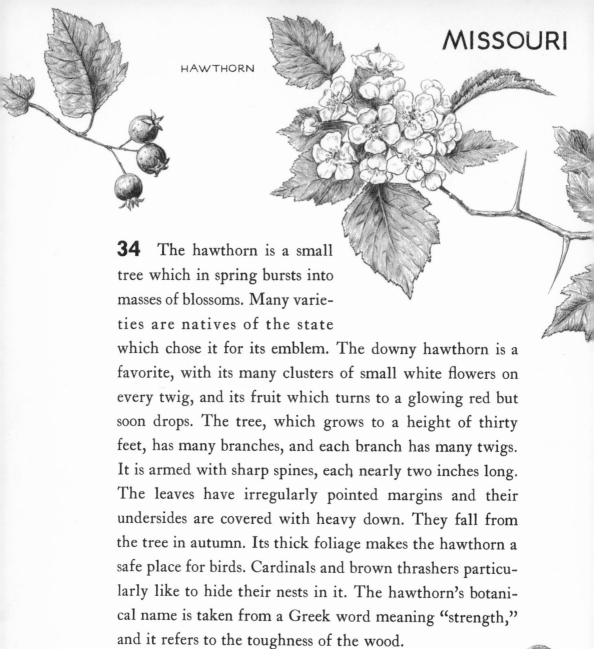

HAWTHORN

**34**   The hawthorn is a small tree which in spring bursts into masses of blossoms. Many varieties are natives of the state which chose it for its emblem. The downy hawthorn is a favorite, with its many clusters of small white flowers on every twig, and its fruit which turns to a glowing red but soon drops. The tree, which grows to a height of thirty feet, has many branches, and each branch has many twigs. It is armed with sharp spines, each nearly two inches long. The leaves have irregularly pointed margins and their undersides are covered with heavy down. They fall from the tree in autumn. Its thick foliage makes the hawthorn a safe place for birds. Cardinals and brown thrashers particularly like to hide their nests in it. The hawthorn's botanical name is taken from a Greek word meaning "strength," and it refers to the toughness of the wood.

Bird: *Bluebird. See page 43.*

Jefferson City

The bitter-root was used by the Indians as a food. The **35** thick branched root is best if it is dug up at flowering time in the spring, when its bitter bark can be easily slipped off. The starchy root is nutritious, and after it is boiled there is little bitter taste. The roots are very long-lived, and even if they are kept out of the soil for several years, they will begin to grow again when they are replanted. The short leaves, shaped like a pencil, are thick and fleshy. The flowers grow close to the ground on stalks only three or four inches long. They are shades of bright rosy red and have many petals. The colored sepals seem like extra petals, for they do not fall off when the blossom opens to its two-inch width. In the bottom of the flower cup there are numerous stamens and the pistil, which separates into six or eight parts. The plant prefers to grow wild in dry soil or gravel, but it can adapt itself to sunny rock gardens. The bitter-root has given its name to a river, a valley, and a mountain range.

Bird: *Western meadowlark. See page 36.*

BITTER-ROOT

⊙Helena

# NEBRASKA

*also*

KANSAS
MONTANA
N. DAKOTA
OREGON
WYOMING

Lincoln

**36** The Western meadowlark differs from the Eastern variety by being paler in the streaked brown of the upper plumage and having a narrower black breast crescent. Bright yellow spreads over the cheeks and colors the under parts of the bird. When in flight, the white feathers in the short tail are very noticeable. This popular bird is a wonderful singer of long, clear, warbling melodies. He is also valued as a destroyer of harmful insects and weed seeds. The "lark of the West" has strong legs and large feet. He makes good use of them, for he spends many hours a day walking slowly through meadows and open fields in search of food. The nest is well hidden beside a tuft of grass. It has an arched roof of grasses. The entrance, in the side of this hideout with its three to seven eggs, is sometimes approached by the birds through a concealed runway. Meadowlarks are not true larks. They are closely related to blackbirds and orioles.

Flower: Goldenrod. See page 24.

WESTERN MEADOWLARK
10¾ inches

**MOUNTAIN
BLUEBIRD**
*7¼ inches*

*also* IDAHO

Sagebrush thrives **37** in dry regions and is the most common plant in the desert. It is a shrubby plant, and may reach its full growth when it is only a foot high or may grow to a height of twelve feet. The upper leaves are much narrower than the lower, which may have from three to five lobes. All are covered with silvery down. Flowering stems grow at the end of the shrub's branches. The tiny florets are grouped in small heads, one eighth of an inch across. These are set tightly against the stem and form inconspicuous yellowish clusters. There is nothing striking about a single sprig of sagebrush, but thousands of the plants, reflecting the day's differing lights, beautify the desert. Several varieties of sagebrush grow on the Western plains, and some of them are useful as winter food for sheep. They also make valuable fuel.

The male mountain bluebird is all blue. The female has bright blue wings and tail, but the rest of her plumage is brownish. Otherwise the bird is similar to the Eastern bluebird.

SAGEBRUSH

*Carson City*

PURPLE FINCH
6¼ inches

**38** The purple finch does not quite live up to his name, for while his head, throat, breast, and lower back are reddish-plum color, the rest of his plumage is either streaked brown or gray white. The female does not have a single "purple" feather. Her general color is gray brown, and she might easily be taken for a sparrow. The melodious spring song of the purple finch, as well as his rich coloring, has made him famous. He sings from the topmost branch of a favorite cedar. Then up and up in the air he flies, without a pause in his song. These sturdy birds are content with a rather shallow, frail nest. It may be six or it may be thirty feet from the ground, in an evergreen tree. They use fine twigs, strips of bark, and other pliable material, and they line the nest with hair. There are four to six eggs and sometimes two broods are reared in a season.

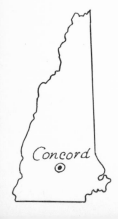

Concord
◉

Purple lilac flowers grow in *panicles*, the botanical **39** name for these pyramid-shaped clusters. The panicles grow at the end of the small branches of a shrub or small tree which may reach twenty feet in height. In the spring lilac bushes are laden with fragrant clusters of flowers. The sizes of the clusters vary. Each individual flower is less than half an inch across; it is a nectar-producing tube, spreading out with a four-pointed star effect. The heart-shaped green leaves are deciduous—that is, they fall off in the autumn. The common purple lilac is found in eastern Europe, but until the early settlers brought plants and seeds here, there were none in this country. Now it is found in almost every garden where the winters are cold enough to suit it. Purple lilacs have also become runaways and grow along roads and on uncared-for land. They prefer a rich soil but survive almost anywhere. They are very long-lived plants.

PURPLE LILAC

# NEW JERSEY

Trenton

**40** The goldfinch's sweet joyful song and the bright lemon yellow of his spring and summer feathers are the reasons for his extra name, wild canary. He has a black cap, worn tipped over his eyes, and his wings and tail are black, marked with white. In autumn, the male is more like the female and the young birds. They are olive brownish above and yellowish white below. Goldfinches delay nest building until late in the season. Perhaps they are waiting for thistledown to be available, for the female likes to pack it, in pads about an inch and a half thick, in the bottom of her little nest, which is carefully woven of bark shreds and grasses. She usually builds in a bush or sapling. The male bird feeds his mate while she is sitting on the four or five bluish eggs. He also helps feed the young birds on seeds that he first partially digests. When their families are reared, the birds live in flocks. They sing as they fly from a weed patch to a seed-bearing tree.

Flower: *Violet.* See page 63.

GOLDFINCH
*5 inches*

*also*
IOWA
MINNESOTA
WASHINGTON

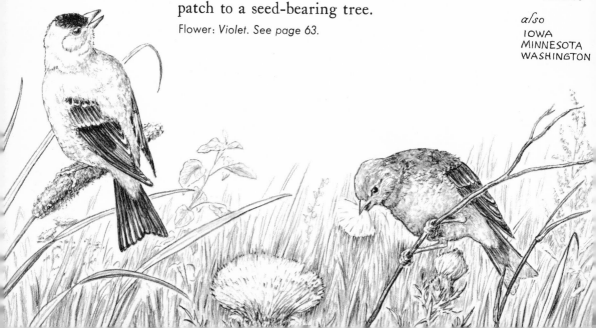

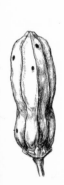

Santa Fé

The yucca grows in **41** various forms, but all types have pointed evergreen leaves which, in dry areas, act as storage vessels for water. The flowers range in color from white or cream to greenish yellow. They are bell-shaped, and great numbers of them hang from a branching stalk which grows from the rosette of leaves. There would be no yuccas if there were no yucca moths, and no yucca moths if there were no yucca flowers. When the plants begin to bloom, the moths suddenly appear. In the evening and throughout the night the female is busy. She flies to an opened flower and collects pollen from its stamens. She packs it like a ball and flies with it to another flower. There, with her egg depositor, she pierces a hole and lays an egg in the seed container. That done, she climbs to the top of the pistil and rams her pollen ball far down into the stigma opening. She seems to know that this will insure the growth of the seeds that will be food for the tiny larva when it hatches from the egg. The larva does not eat more than one quarter of the seeds and then it bores its way out. Several ripe pods may show more than one exit hole.

YUCCA

NEW MEXICO

**42** The road runner, when he races swiftly across the desert, leaves peculiar tracks in the soil. His large foot has two toes in front and two behind, and it is sometimes hard to tell which way he has traveled. This toe arrangement earns him his extra name of ground cuckoo. It is said that in the horse-and-buggy days the bird delighted in running along the road ahead of vehicles. If he wants to stop suddenly, the road runner puts on the brakes by erecting and spreading his tail. The plumage of male and female is similar. Coarse and harsh, it is various shades of buff, brown, bluish black, white, bronze, and green. Bare skin around the eyes is colored blue and orange. The bird enjoys meals of lizards, snakes, centipedes, large insects, and mice. The nest, usually in cactus or some thorny bush, is made of sticks and weed stalks and is lined with root fiber, snake skin, and feathers. The four to six young birds hatch at intervals, and the first may be well grown before the last is out of the egg.

ROAD RUNNER
20 to 24 inches

The Eastern **43** bluebird is a flashing vivid blue. The color is due to refraction rather than pigment in his feathers, and he looks his bluest in bright sunlight. The blue is set off by a rosy-chestnut breast shading to white under parts. The female is much duller in color, with her grayish-blue back and her breast just tinged with red brown. Though they often nest in holes in apple trees or other trees, bluebirds seem to prefer to build in man-made boxes. Year after year a pair will return to the same nesting box, which they line each season with grass and weed stalks. They use fine grass as a cushion on which to hatch the four to six bluish-white eggs. The bluebird's voice is a cheerful soft warble, and he does no harm except to the insects on which he feeds. He also eats wild berries. Some of the birds spend the winter in the Gulf States; others stay north in some sheltered area. The bluebird belongs to the thrush family. Young bluebirds, like thrushes, have spotted breasts.

Flower: *Wild rose. See page 22.*

BLUEBIRD
*7 inches*

*also* MISSOURI

*Albany*

# NORTH CAROLINA

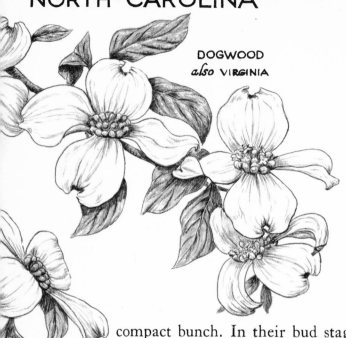

**DOGWOOD**
*also* VIRGINIA

**44** The dogwood is a shrub or small tree, with spreading branches. In the spring, it is covered with a mass of "flowers." Actually, these are bracts and not flowers. Dogwood flowers are very tiny and greenish yellow, and they grow in a compact bunch. In their bud stage, during the preceding winter, the group is protected by four small brown bracts which cover them snugly. When the winter is over, these bracts begin to grow and to change color, until finally they reach a width of three or four inches and are white or pale pink. Then the inconspicuous true flowers open their four petals for visiting insects. At the time the bracts put on their display, very few of the tree's green leaves have unfolded. In the autumn dogwood foliage turns rich shades of red and the fruit turns scarlet. The leaves fall, but the berries linger through winter snows. Dogwood thrives in woods under larger trees or in sunny exposed places.

*Bird: Cardinal. See pages 20 and 62.*

*Raleigh*

The prairie rose, with stems from six to fifteen feet **45** long, climbs over walls and fences. It also grows in the open as a bush, with the stems growing upright for half their length and then arching downward. The stems have a scattering of curved thorns. The leaves have three or occasionally five leaflets. Narrow leaflets, known as bracts, grow where the stalk of the leaf joins the stem. This wild rose blooms in early summer. The flowers grow in a loose cluster, with more buds opening as the earlier blossoms fade. Prairie roses are deep pink when they open, and change to white when full-blown. Numerous yellow stamens surround the pistils, which form a column in the flower's center. After the rose withers, the urn-shaped seed container, formed by the sepals joined together, slowly turns red. The prairie rose has underground stems, called rhizomes or rootstocks. They spread widely, running along about a foot below the surface of the ground. With intervals between them, new shoots grow up and new roots grow down, and a new rosebush comes into the world.

Bird: *Western meadowlark. See page 36.*

Bismarck
⊙

PRAIRIE ROSE

# OHIO

**46** The red carnation was honored with the title of state flower of Ohio in memory of President William McKinley. He was born in Niles, Ohio, in 1843, and it was his favorite flower. More than one hundred varieties of carnations have been developed by man from the original wild pink, which had only five petals. Carnations now have a great number of fringed petals, which taper to a narrow stalk. These stalks are held together in a tight bunch by a tubular five-pointed calyx. As the ovary grows, deep down in the tube, the calyx splits and the petals spill outward through its side. The stem of the flower and the leaves are a soft gray green and have a waxy bloom. The leaves are long and narrow and their shape is called linear by botanists. Each pair of leaves is set very close to the pair below it, and they grow in groups like an upright tassel. Carnations come in many colors. Some of them have a narrow edging of a second color trimming the petals. The flowers are very fragrant. Commercial growers often raise carnations in hothouses. The plant then grows to a height of three feet.

Bird: *Cardinal. See pages 20 and 62.*

RED
CARNATION

Columbus

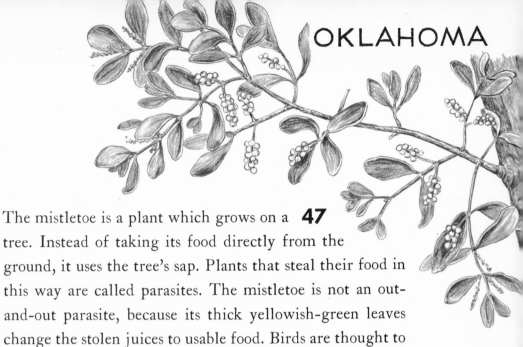

The mistletoe is a plant which grows on a **47** tree. Instead of taking its food directly from the ground, it uses the tree's sap. Plants that steal their food in this way are called parasites. The mistletoe is not an out-and-out parasite, because its thick yellowish-green leaves change the stolen juices to usable food. Birds are thought to plant the sticky seeds when, having feasted on the creamy-white berries, they wipe their bills on the bark of a tree. The seed, stuck in a crevice of a branch, sprouts. Roots penetrate the bark and a new mistletoe plant begins its slow growth. The thickly branched clump may be three feet or more across. The flowers, borne on short spikes, are very small and inconspicuous.

MISTLETOE

The scissor-tailed flycatcher is a useful, handsome bird. His streaming forked tail may take up ten inches of his fourteen-inch length. He scissors it open and shut in his erratic flight. He eats many harmful insects.

Oklahoma
⊙ City

SCISSOR-TAILED
FLYCATCHER
14 inches

# OREGON

**48** The Oregon grape or holly grape, as the shrub is often called, is a close relative of the barberries—a large family whose members are found in many parts of the world. The Oregon grape grows abundantly on the foothills and mountainsides of the Northwest. The evergreen plant, which has woody branching stems, grows to a height of six feet. There are varying numbers of hollylike leaflets to each leaf. The leaflets are well armed, for their edges have sharp spines pointing in every direction. The new leaves are pale green early in the season, but soon become a shining dark green. In the autumn the foliage takes on rich shades of bronze and red. In the spring many erect clusters of small yellow flowers come into bloom near the ends of the branches. The clusters are about three inches long. By autumn the fruit has developed into grapelike bunches of bright blue-purple berries. The fruit is edible, and sometimes jelly is made from it.

Bird: *Western meadowlark. See page 36.*

OREGON GRAPE

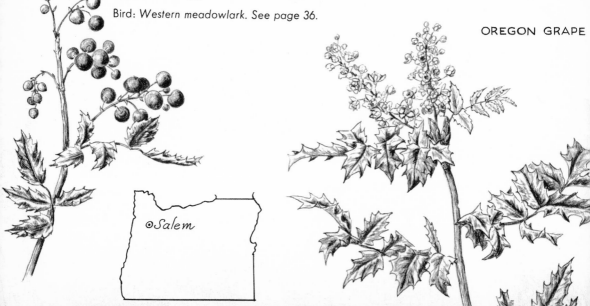

⊙*Salem*

# PENNSYLVANIA

Harrisburg ◎

The ruffed grouse is a very hand- **49** some bird. His feathers are all shades of brown, from a rich red brown to a golden brown, blended with a yellowish white. His ruff is purplish black. The male ruffed grouse has the remarkable habit of "drumming." Standing very upright on a log, he beats his wings against the air with such speedy vibrations that they are just a blur. The result is a drumming sound that can be heard a mile away. He drums to call his mate. He drums as a challenge to other males. Sometimes he drums just for the fun of it. The nest is on the ground, usually beside a sheltering log or stump. It is found in the woods often near a trail. So closely does the color of the sitting female match the surrounding dry leaves that she is practically invisible. The eight to fourteen young birds leave the nest shortly after they break from the egg. Quickly they learn to feed themselves. Ruffed grouse eat leaf buds, berries, other plant food, and insects. In the winter, hornlike fringes sprout on each toe, and these serve the bird as snowshoes. They are shed in the spring.

Flower: *Mountain laurel. See page 14.*

RUFFED GROUSE
*18 inches*

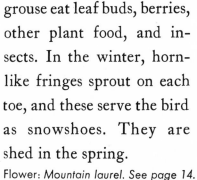

# RHODE ISLAND

*Providence*

**50** The Rhode Island Red has been a famous fowl for many years. The birds are extremely hardy and are excellent for table use. The hen is a good producer of eggs. This bird can claim the red Malay gamecock as one of his ancestors. The plumage is a rich reddish color, set off by black in the tail feathers and on the wings. One subvariety has a large comb on the top of his head, and the other has a smaller decoration. Like all birds, they have an oil gland at the base of the tail. When the bird preens, oil is transferred to the feathers in order to rainproof them. Newly hatched chicks are covered with soft down and need protection in bad weather.

Flower: *Violet. See page 63.*

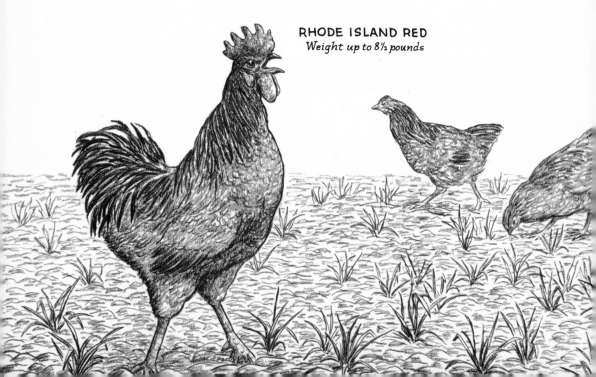

**RHODE ISLAND RED**
*Weight up to 8½ pounds*

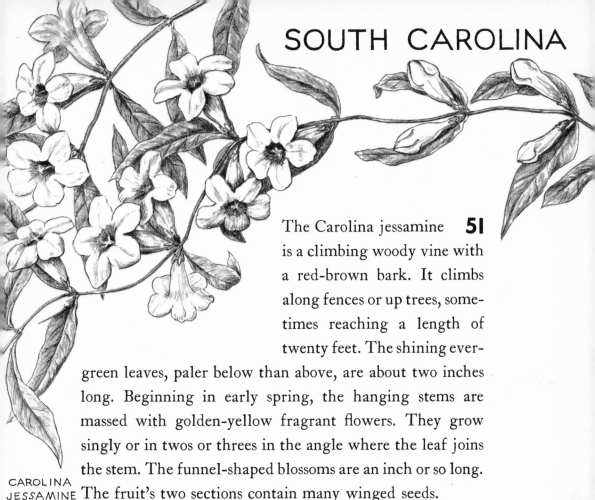

The Carolina jessamine **51** is a climbing woody vine with a red-brown bark. It climbs along fences or up trees, sometimes reaching a length of twenty feet. The shining evergreen leaves, paler below than above, are about two inches long. Beginning in early spring, the hanging stems are massed with golden-yellow fragrant flowers. They grow singly or in twos or threes in the angle where the leaf joins the stem. The funnel-shaped blossoms are an inch or so long. The fruit's two sections contain many winged seeds.

CAROLINA JESSAMINE

The Carolina wren is admired for his voice and his energy. He sings in all seasons and in all weather. His tail is in constant motion as he darts about eagerly hunting for insects and berries. In color, he is rusty brown above and dull buffy white below. He has a conspicuous white stripe over his eye. He is also known as the mocking wren.

Columbia

CAROLINA WREN
5¾ inches

# SOUTH DAKOTA

**52** The pasque flower is thought to have been given its name either because it blooms in early spring, or because dye made from the plant was used for coloring Easter eggs. Pasque means Passover or Easter. The flower has no true petals. Instead, it has inch-long sepals. These are colored so that they resemble petals. They are bluish purple and surround the numerous stamens and pistils. The many seed capsules form a compact head and, as they develop, the pistils grow into feathery plumes about two inches long. They give the ripened seed head the appearance of a fluffy ball. When the flower fades its stalk begins to grow, raising the seed head several inches. This stalk lengthening is a habit among the anemones, which are near kin to the pasque flowers. The whole plant is covered with long silky hairs, and it grows up to a foot in height. The furry leaves, with deeply split edges, grow directly from the tuberous root. They appear when the flowers have faded. The pasque flower likes prairie lands and dry soil.

PASQUE FLOWER

Pierre

The ring-necked pheasant was imported from China. **53**
The birds made themselves at home here about 1880 after
several earlier attempts to naturalize them had failed. The
general plumage of the male is a rich mixture of browns and
shades of golden buff, barred with black. The head, bare and
scarlet at the sides, and the neck are feathered in peacock blue
with reflected purple and bronze lights. The ring neck is the
collar of white feathers. The female is plainly dressed in
shades of brown. Pheasants are good to eat and weigh three
or more pounds; often they are raised on farms and then released. In the wild state, these dignified birds fearlessly for-
age in open fields for insect and plant food. In the hunting
season they sensibly prefer to stay near thickets or in the
woods. Partly sheltered by dry grass or a tuft of weeds, the
nest is a depression made in dry leaves. As many as thirteen
chicks may be hatched and they leave the nest within twenty-
four hours.

# SOUTH DAKOTA

# TENNESSEE

*Nashville*

**54**   The iris, which varies in height, size, and color, has a flower stalk growing from a flat fanlike set of leaves, shaped like swords. The flower has three petals and three sepals, and the style of the pistil is divided into three branches. The arrangement of these parts is peculiar and their duties unusual. A bee, instead of settling on the petals that arch upward from the flower's center, uses the broad sepals as a landing place. The sepals curve downward and have honey-guide markings and sometimes golden "beards." Over each sepal there is a wide flat branch of the pistil. This forms a tunnel. Along its roof is the pollen-bearing stamen and under its entrance arch is the stigma. To reach the nectar, a bee must go through the tunnel. Pollen sticks to its back and is later carried to another flower, for the stigma is so placed that it cannot receive pollen from a departing insect. Iris grows from a rootstock which is often partly above the surface of the soil.
Bird: *Mockingbird. See page 9.*

IRIS

The bluebonnet grows only in Texas. It is **55** one of many species of wild lupines, a name derived from a Latin word meaning wolf. It was once thought that, because the plant grows on dry or waste land, it "ate" the soil. Its long roots enable it to thrive, and actually lupines do good to the soil rather than harm. The flowers, appearing in the spring, are bright blue violet. They grow in a long cluster on a stem about a foot in height. The stem, as well as the underside of each leaf, which is made up of five leaflets, is covered with silky hairs. The blossom has a banner petal, marked with a spot, and two side petals which conceal two inner ones that are shaped like the keel of a boat. These protect the stamens and pistil. When a bee alights on the side petals, the keel spreads, enabling the insect to reach the pollen and nectar. The oblong seed pod is very hairy. Lupine leaves sleep at night. In some species, the leaflets droop around their stem, while in others the whole leaf points upward.

The Western mockingbird has a little more white on his wings and is very slightly larger than the "mocker" of the East, described on Page 9.

BLUEBONNET

Austin

WESTERN MOCKINGBIRD

# UTAH

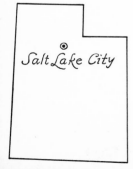

**56**  The sego lily has been in favor ever since the days of the early Mormon settlers. They found that the bulblike roots of the plant were a satisfactory addition to their dwindling store of food. The sego lily grows from a short bulblike fleshy stem which grows underground, called a corm. The plant's few bluish-green leaves are long and narrow. The flowers are about two inches across, and two or three of them may be borne on the stiff slender stem. They have three petals and three sepals. In coloring, the flowers show great variety. The white petals may be tinged with yellow, green, or lilac. Near their base they are decorated with a yellow heart, edged with purple. The sepals are colorfully tinted also. Its lovely hues and markings have earned this lily the name mariposa, a Spanish word meaning butterfly. The plants grow in great masses among sagebrush and on the desert. The flowers, on stems one to two feet tall, bloom in the spring. The sego lily belongs to the tulip branch of the lily family.

Salt Lake City

CALIFORNIA
GULL
23 *inches*

The California gull is honored in grateful remem- brance of the saving of the crops planted by the early settlers of Utah. About one hundred years ago, millions of black crickets appeared in three successive seasons and destroyed all growing plants. Starvation was near. Then the gulls came. They ate every last cricket and the crops were saved. The glistening white adult birds have a mantle of blue-gray feathers over the back and wings. The long feathers of the wings are black marked with white. There is a bright red spot on the lower bill and a black dot on the upper. Until their third year, the plumage of the young gulls is dusky white with dark markings. California gulls travel in flocks. Usually thought of as birds of the sea, they spend much of their time inland. Colonies of them nest together on the shores of lakes. The eggs, three or four in number, are laid in a nest of small sticks and grasses which is built on the ground.

# VERMONT

Montpelier

**58** The hermit thrush is not always easy to recognize, but he differs from other thrushes in size and color. He has a distinguishing reddish-brown tail, distinctly different from the brown of his back and head. He has light under parts, with chains of brown-black markings on his throat and breast, and a buff-colored eye ring. On the ground, where he feeds, he has a characteristic habit of raising his tail. The "Chek! Chek!" of his alarm call gives no hint of the fluid purity of his flutelike song. He gets his name of "hermit" from his habit of becoming silent when aware of a listener, for this bird is very shy during the breeding season. At the end of the summer he leaves the damp quiet woods and the mountainsides for more southerly winter quarters, and then he is seen more easily. But his singing belongs to his solitude. The loosely built nest is either on the ground or close to it, and three or four blue-green eggs are laid. Hermit thrushes eat berries, and in the summer insects are added to their diet.

HERMIT THRUSH
*7 inches*

Red clover, like other clovers, has a deceptive blos- **59** som. A single globe-shaped clover head is made up of about a hundred florets. The first to come into bloom are those at the base of the head. When the blossoms fade they do not fall off, but turn brown and dry up. Each encloses a seed pod containing one seed. The nectar is in the bottom of the red clover's deep tubular corolla, and only butterflies and bumblebees have tongues long enough to reach it. Butter-flies, with their long slender tongues, can feast without disturbing the pollen. It is the bumblebees that do the work of distributing it. To reach the sweet juice they push open the petals, and in the proc-ess their hairy heads are dusted with pollen. Unknowingly, they carry it to another floret. Bumblebees sometimes cheat by biting a hole low in the corolla tube and using it as a short cut to get at the nectar. Red clover leaves go to sleep at night, with the top leaflet folded over the two side ones. The plant grows to a height of two feet and the flower heads are about one inch across.

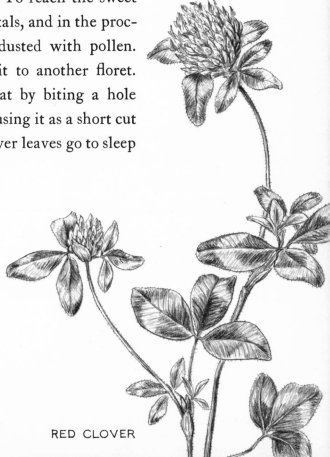

RED CLOVER

# VIRGINIA

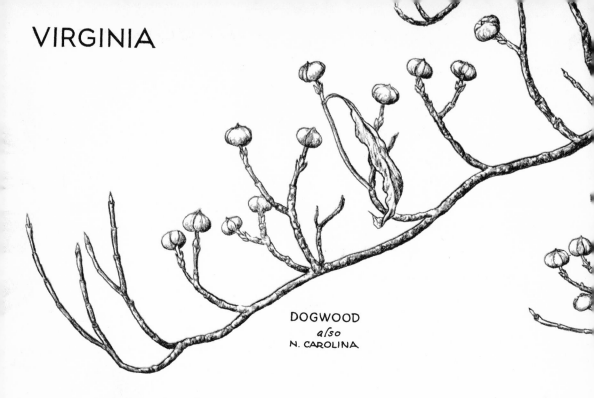

DOGWOOD
also
N. CAROLINA

**60** The American dogwood bears the "flowers" (see page 44) chosen by two states as their emblem. No one is sure how the tree got its name. The dried leaves and the bark of a European species were brewed to make a lotion to cure dogs of mange, and the tree's name perhaps came from this use. In winter the leafless tree is easily recognized, for, in addition to the bunches of scarlet berries it may have, there will be many grayish buttonlike buds on the tips of upcurved twigs. The low-branching tree is seldom more than thirty feet tall.

Bird: *Cardinal. See pages 20 and 62.*

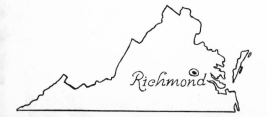

Richmond

WILLOW GOLDFINCH

The rhododendron grows wild in **61** many parts of the world. Though the leaves droop in freezing temperatures, the plants thrive in cold climates. In early summer flowers nearly cover the plant. They are borne in terminal clusters, that is, they grow in groups at the end of a branch. The Coast rhododendron of the West is a shrub some twenty feet in height. The long shining leaves are dark green on top and a paler green underneath. They form a handsome frame for the delicate rosy-purple or pink flowers which have five waxen petals, flecked with greenish and golden spots. The mountain rhododendron of West Virginia is equally beautiful and sometimes grows to be a thirty-five-foot tree. The flowers are usually rose-colored; they are about one and a half inches across, slightly smaller than the Coast variety.

The willow goldfinch is not quite so brightly colored nor quite as big as the Eastern goldfinch described on Page 40. Otherwise the birds are similar.

Olympia

RHODODENDRON

*also* W. VIRGINIA

# WEST VIRGINIA

CARDINAL
*8¾ inches*
*also*
ILLINOIS
INDIANA
KENTUCKY
N. CAROLINA
OHIO
VIRGINIA

**62** The cardinal (see page 20) is favored by more states than any other bird. He is easily identified by his brilliant color and by his musical voice. He seems to enjoy living close to houses, if there are shrubs and thickets nearby. In the winter he is a regular visitor at feeding stations, though he seldom becomes tame. At nesting time he is much less fearful, and frequently he builds his nest within a few feet of a house. Then, regardless of people, he and his mate fly back and forth as they feed the baby birds. The babies leave the nest before they can fly properly. They call constantly from the underbrush, seeming to tell their parents, "Here I am!"

Flower: *Rhododendron. See page 61.*

Charleston

# WISCONSIN

The violet is the chosen emblem of **63** four states. Wisconsin's bird's-foot violet often has upper petals that are a deeper shade of purple than the lower ones. The leaves of this variety are supposed to look like a bird's foot. Most violets have heart-shaped leaves. Though in winter a violet plant seems to disappear, it does not die. The rootstock shrinks, but with the coming of spring it swells and sprouts anew. It is a perennial plant. Violets have five petals—one upper pair and, below them, another pair separated by a broader petal. This center petal is elongated to form a spur, and is wide enough to act as a platform for visiting insects. The honey guides marked on it lead to the nectar in the spur. As the insects feast, pollen brought from another flower is brushed from them. As the flowers fade, the leaves grow taller. In many varieties short-stemmed buds develop, which never open. These closed flowers are self-fertilizing and produce seed. They appear if the regular flowers have set no seeds. The ripe capsule explodes and violet seeds are shot some distance from the plant.

Bird: *Robin. See page 31.*

*also*
ILLINOIS
NEW JERSEY
RHODE ISLAND

BIRD'S·FOOT
VIOLET

*Madison*

# WYOMING

**64**   The Indian paintbrush is one of a group of plants that seem, at first glance, to bear gay flowers, but a closer look shows that appearances are sometimes deceiving. Actually the tubular creamy flowers, about one inch in length, are almost hidden by the sepals, which are tipped with orange red, and the light-red bracts, which are one to two inches long. The real leaves are green. They, and the rest of the plant, are covered with short fine hairs. This member of the figwort family grows to about two feet in height, and near the ground it divides into several stalks which in turn have little branches. The flowers are borne at their tips in long thick clusters. The plant blossoms in early summer, and when the lovely color has gone, its place is taken by the ridged black seed capsules. There are many varieties of paintbrushes, and most of them help themselves to their neighbors' food by sending their roots into those of nearby plants.

Bird: *Western meadowlark. See page 36.*

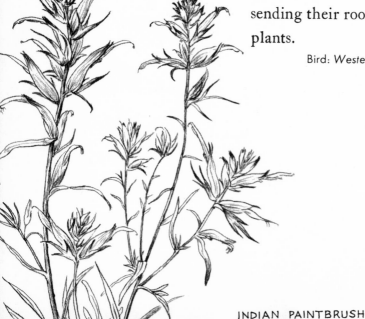

INDIAN PAINTBRUSH

*Cheyenne*